Poliziotto su Patrol
Libro da colorare

Coloring Pages for Kids

Coloring Pages for Kids
An imprint of Ciparum LLC

Poliziotto su Patrol Libro da colorare
© 2017 Ciparum LLC
All rights reserved.
ISBN-10:1-63589-352-6
ISBN-13:978-1-63589-352-6

Coloring Pages for Kids

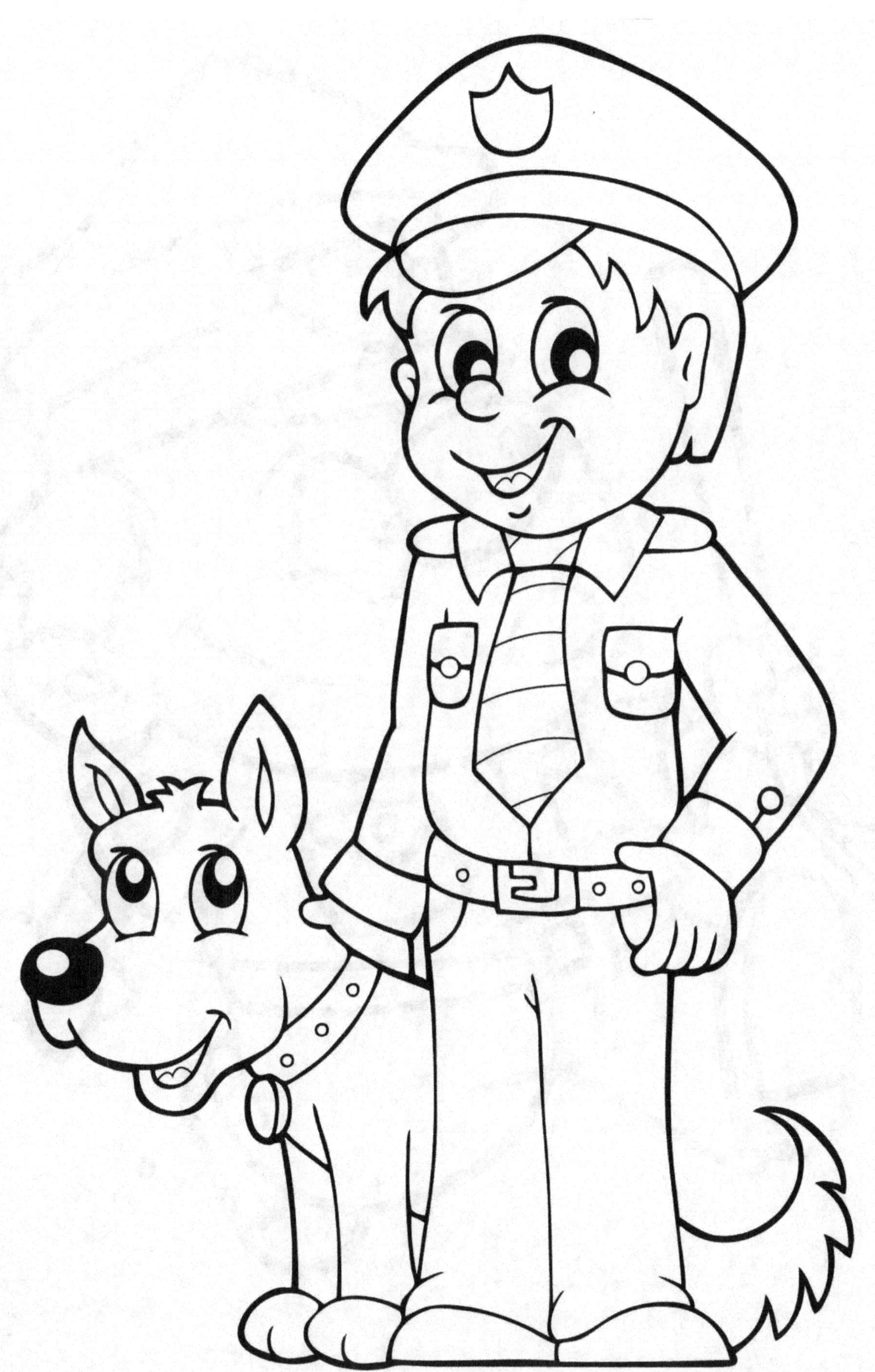

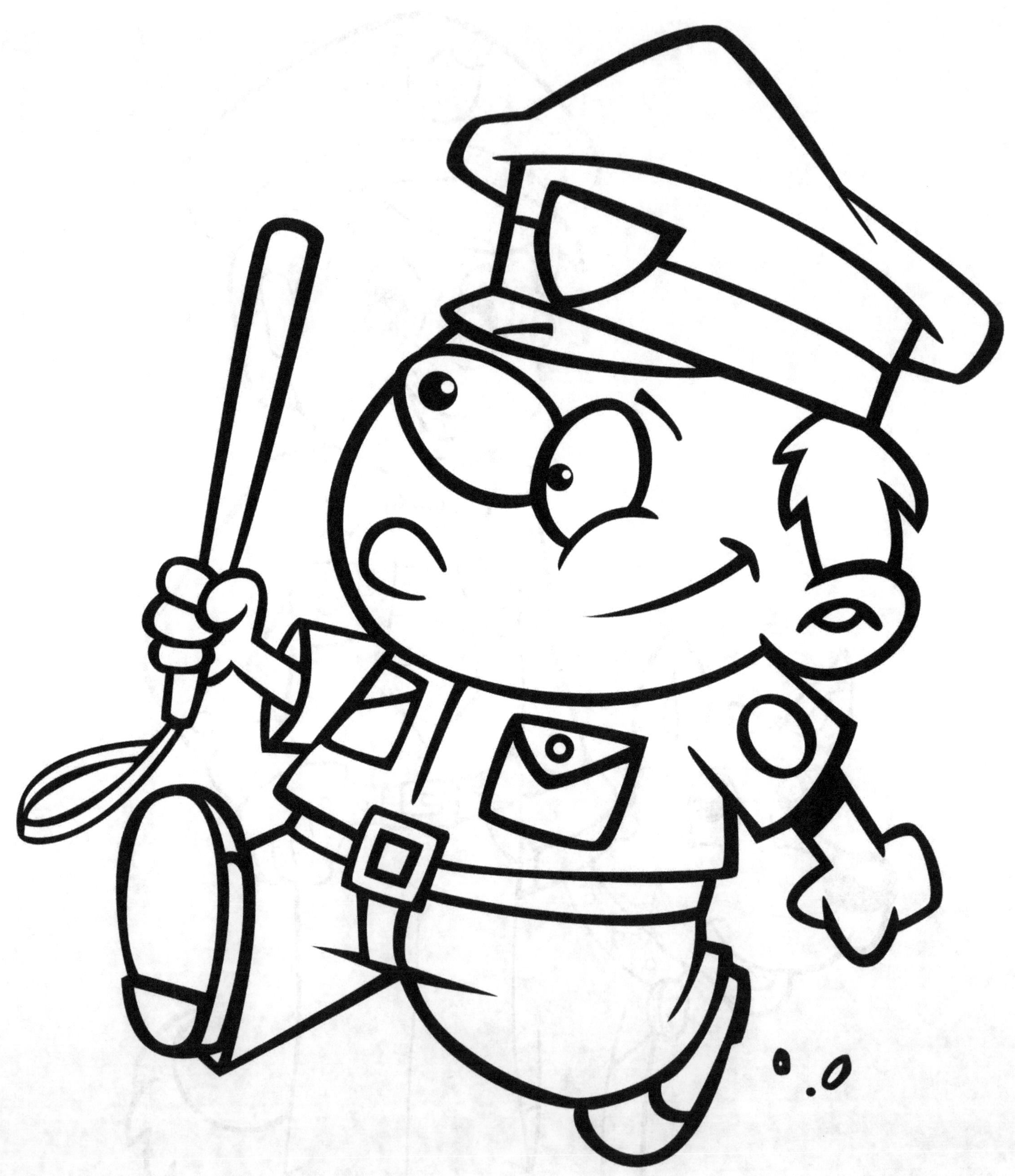

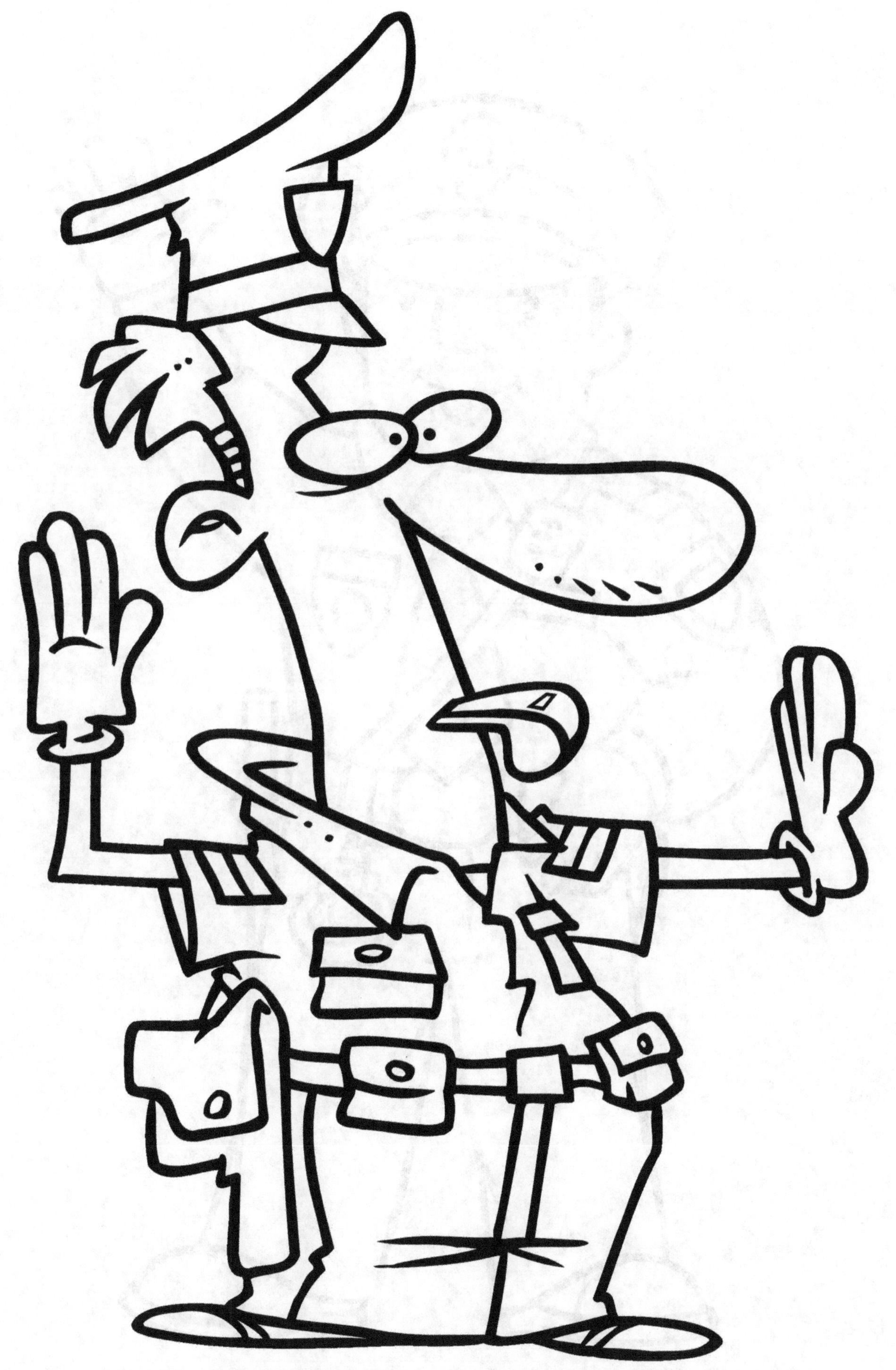

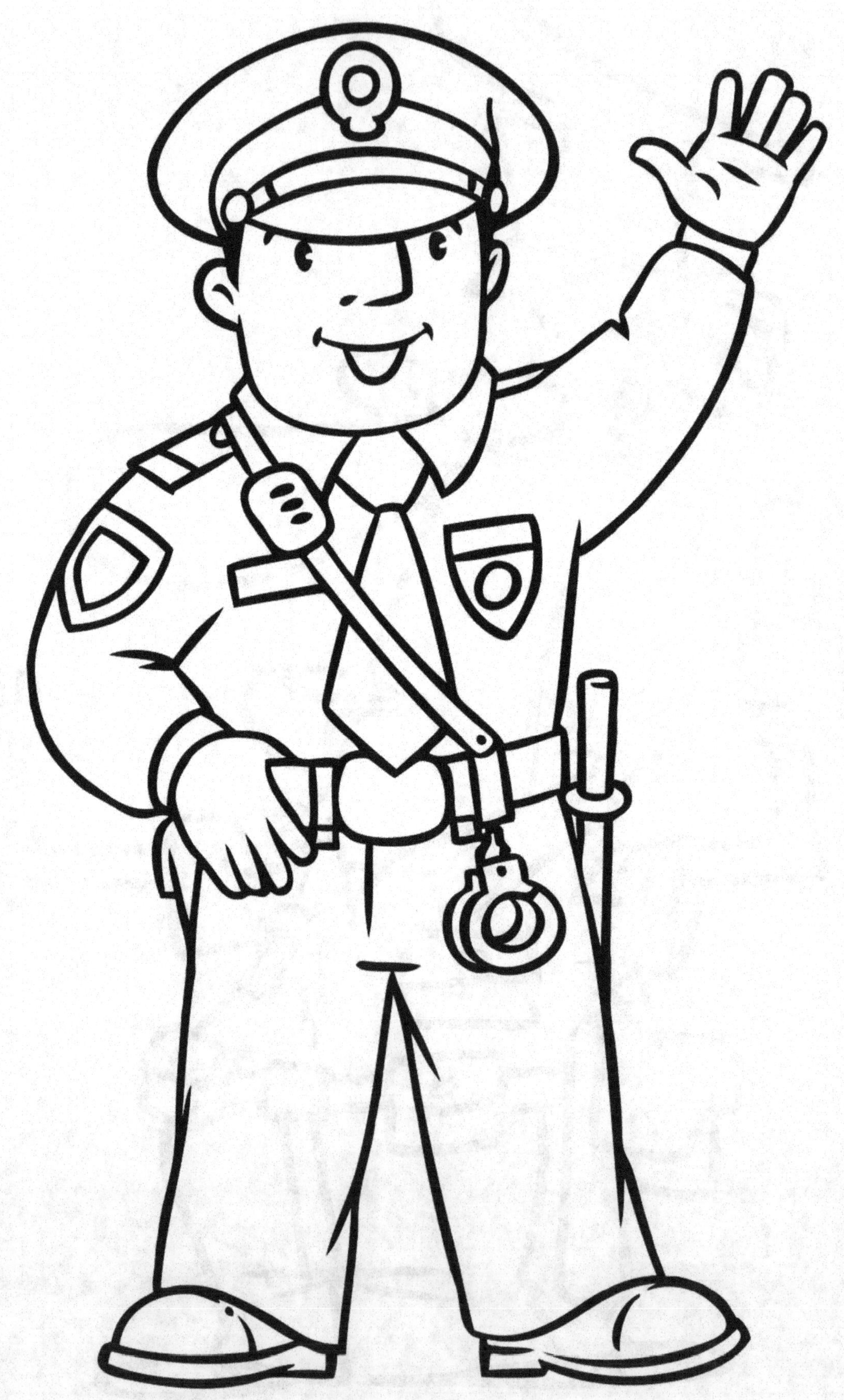

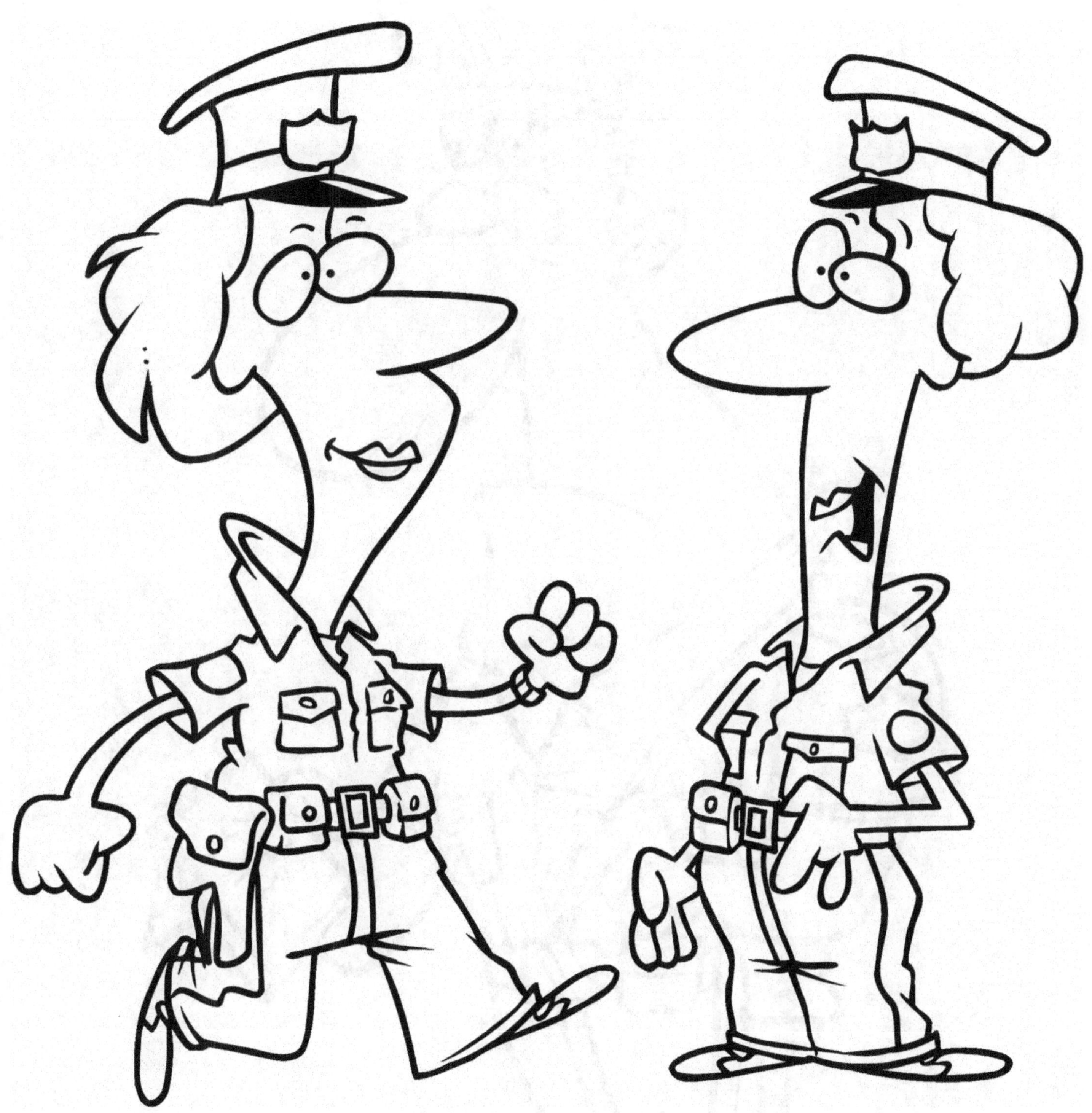

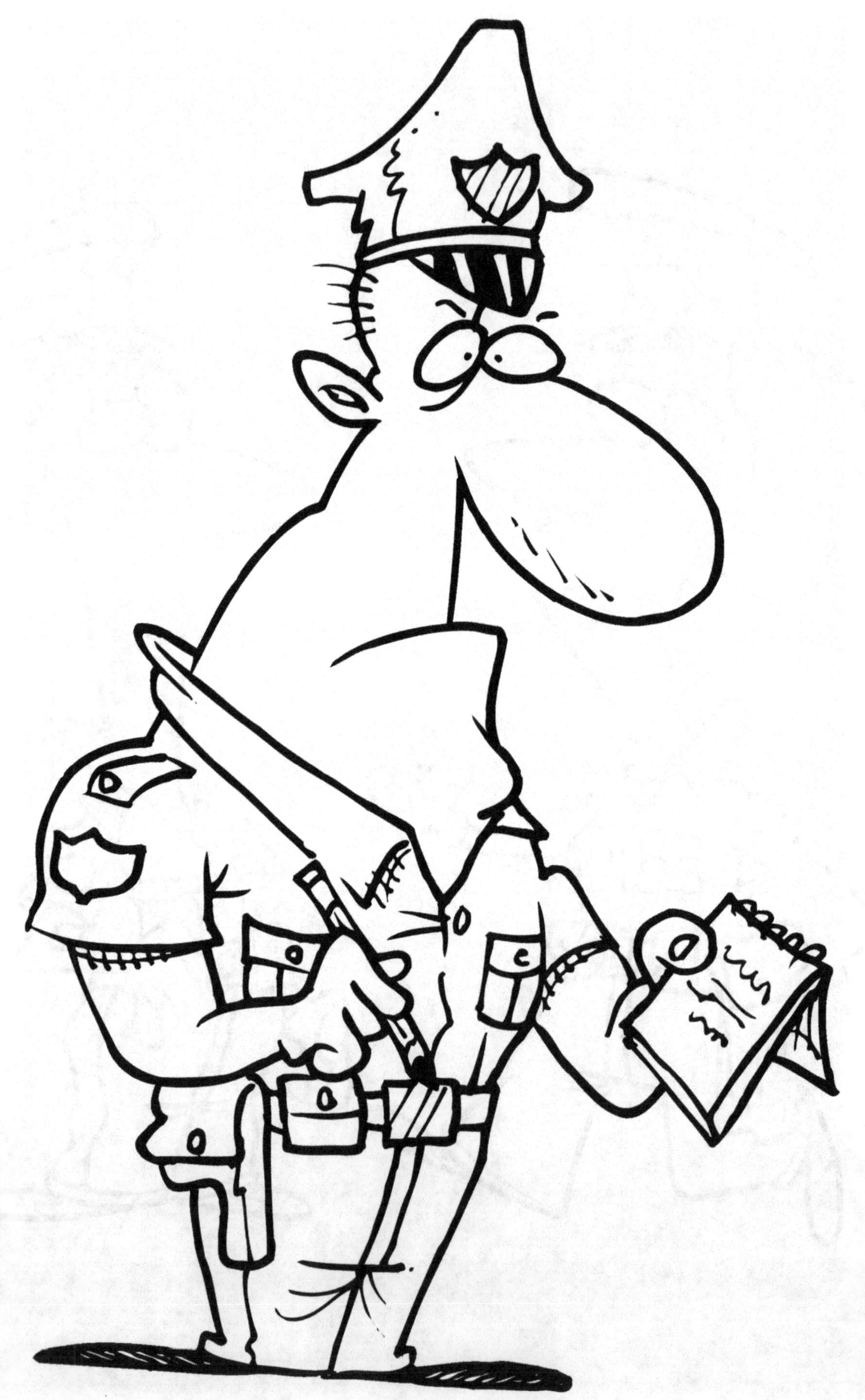

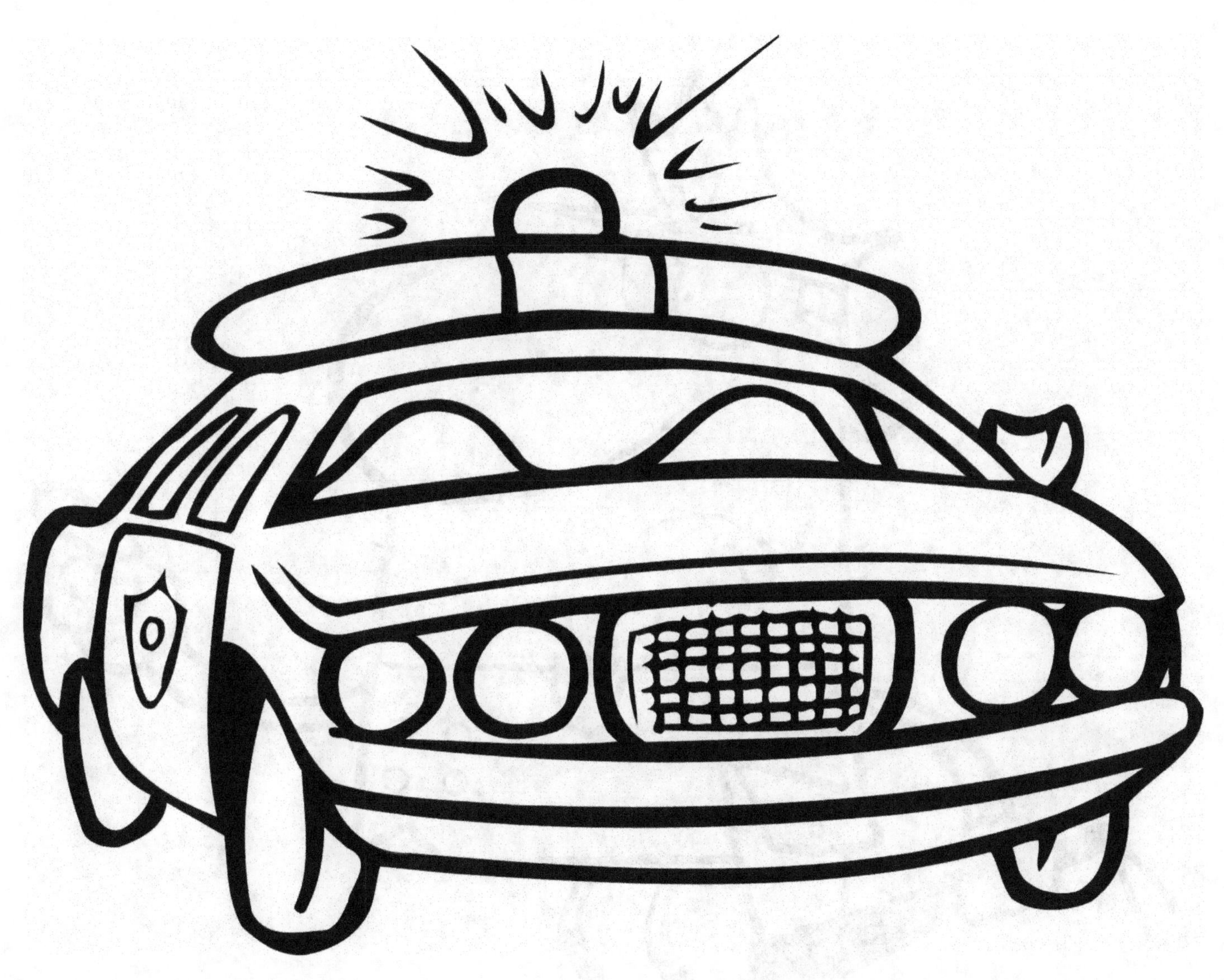

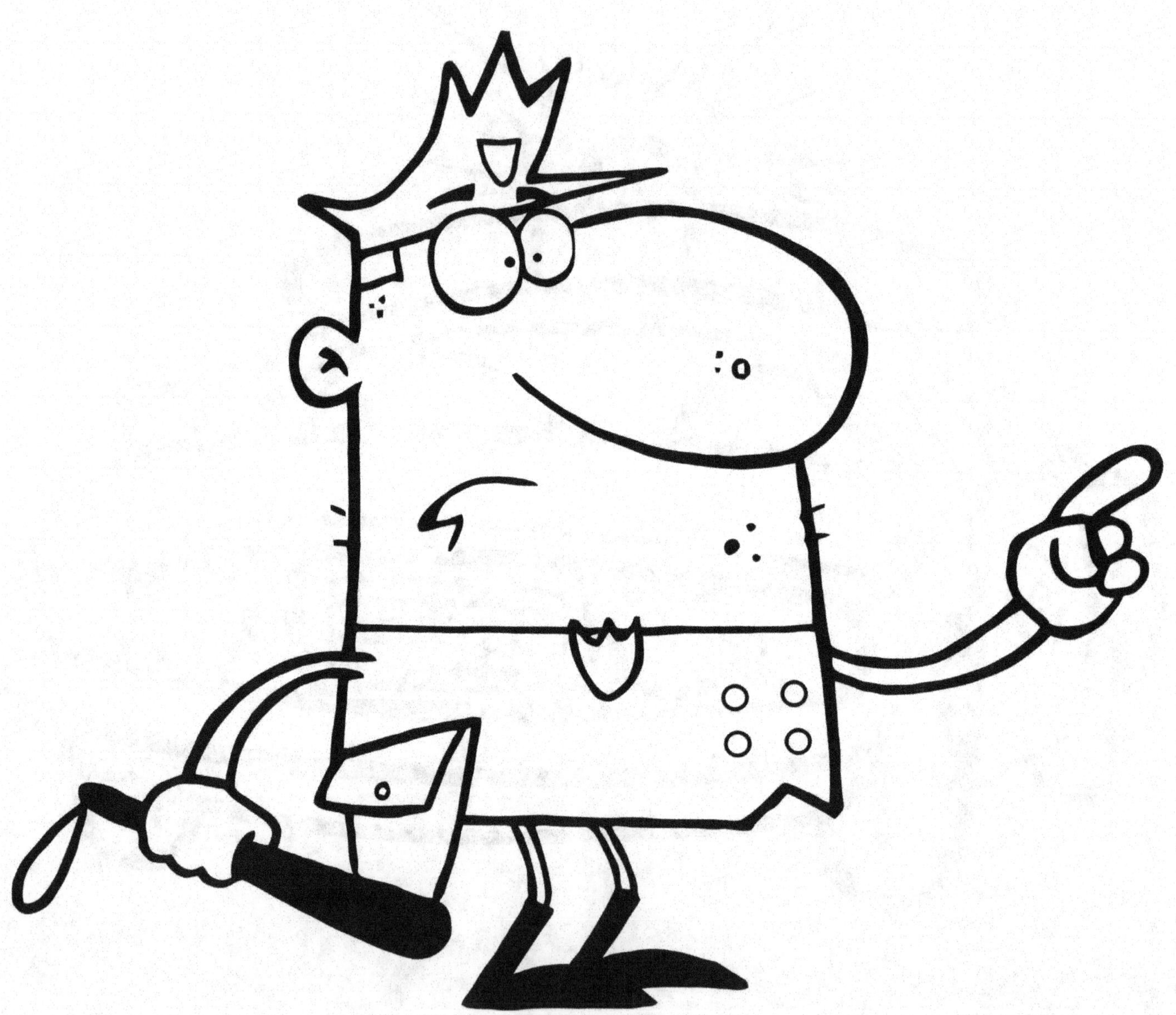

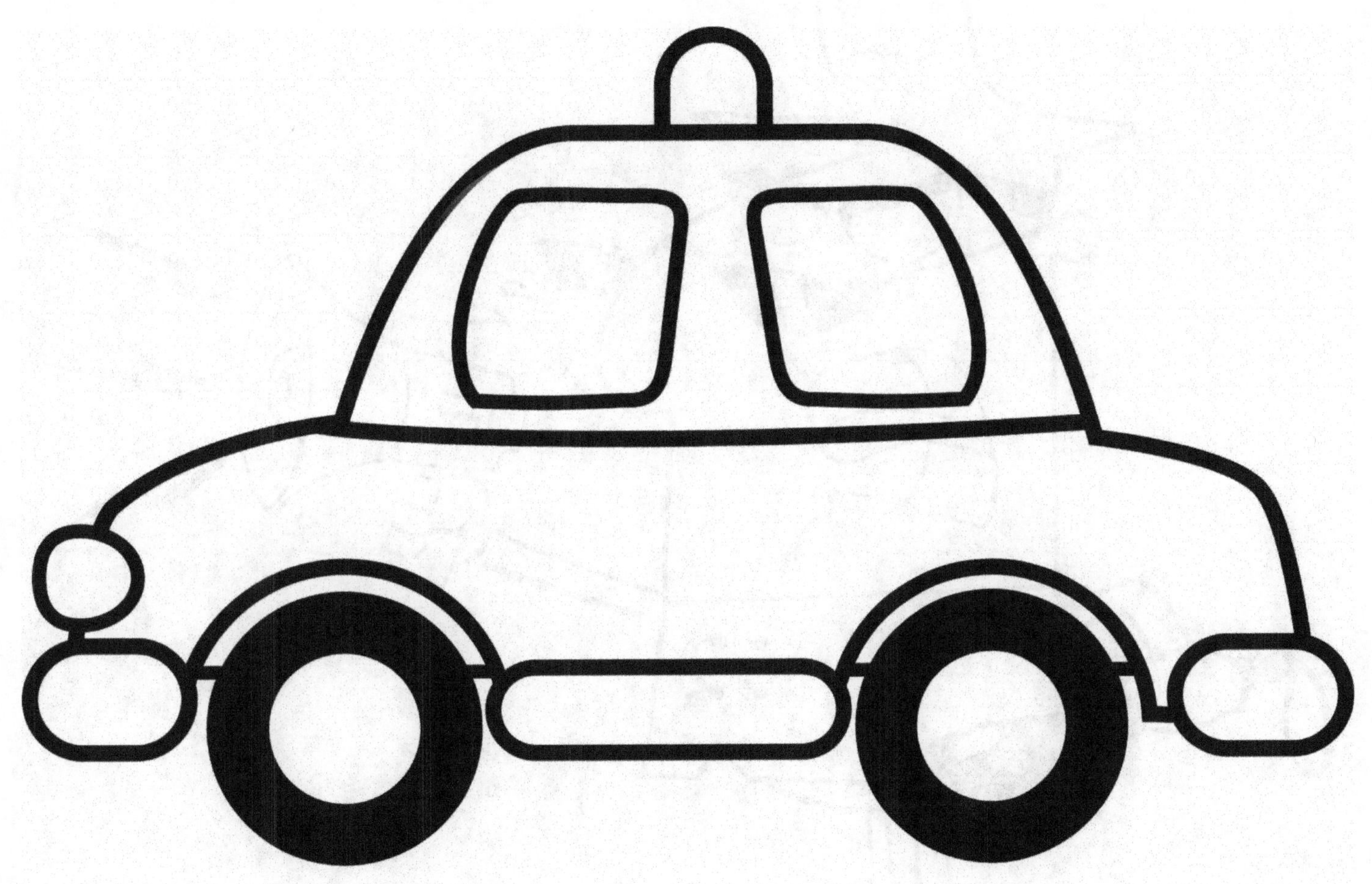

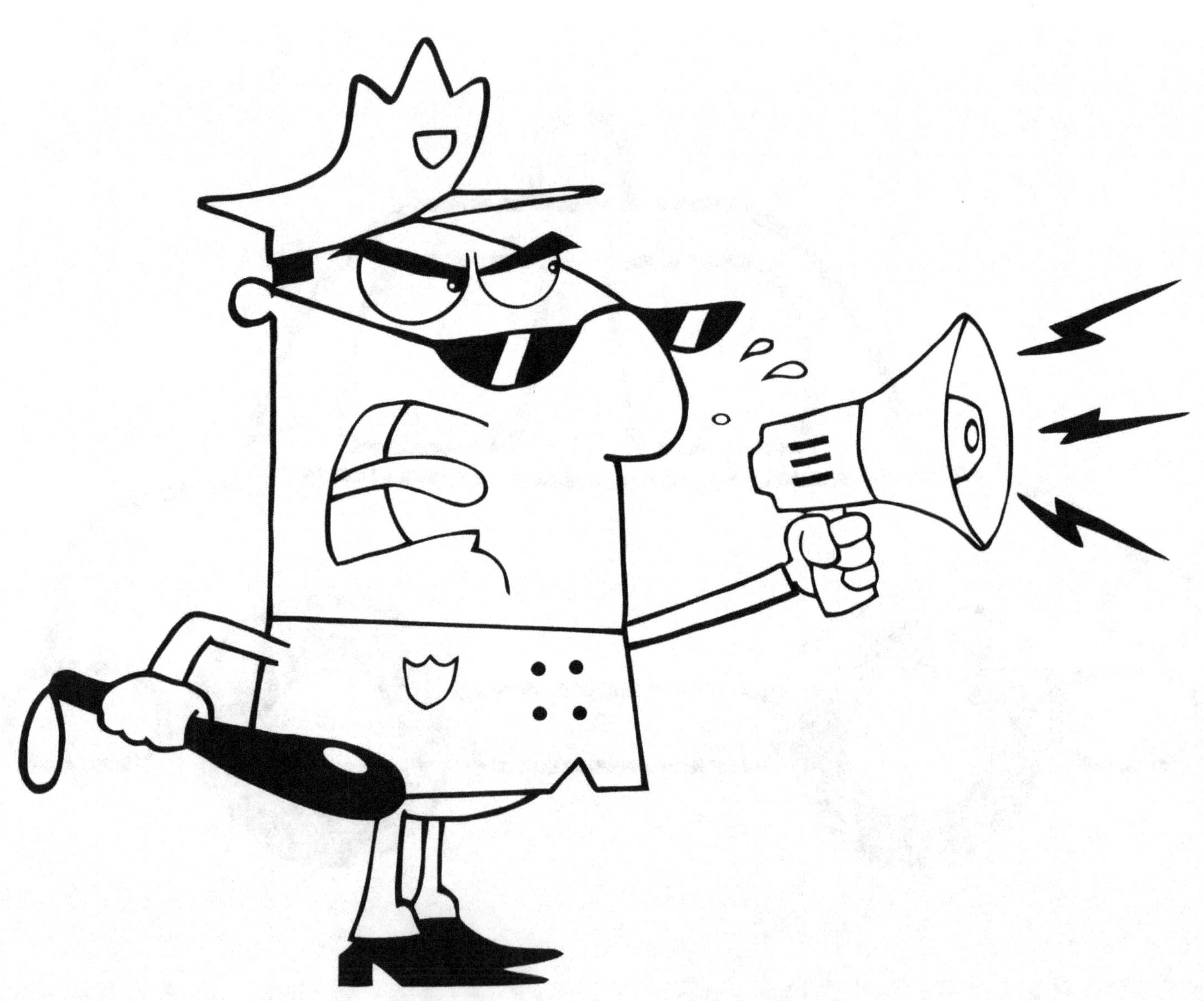

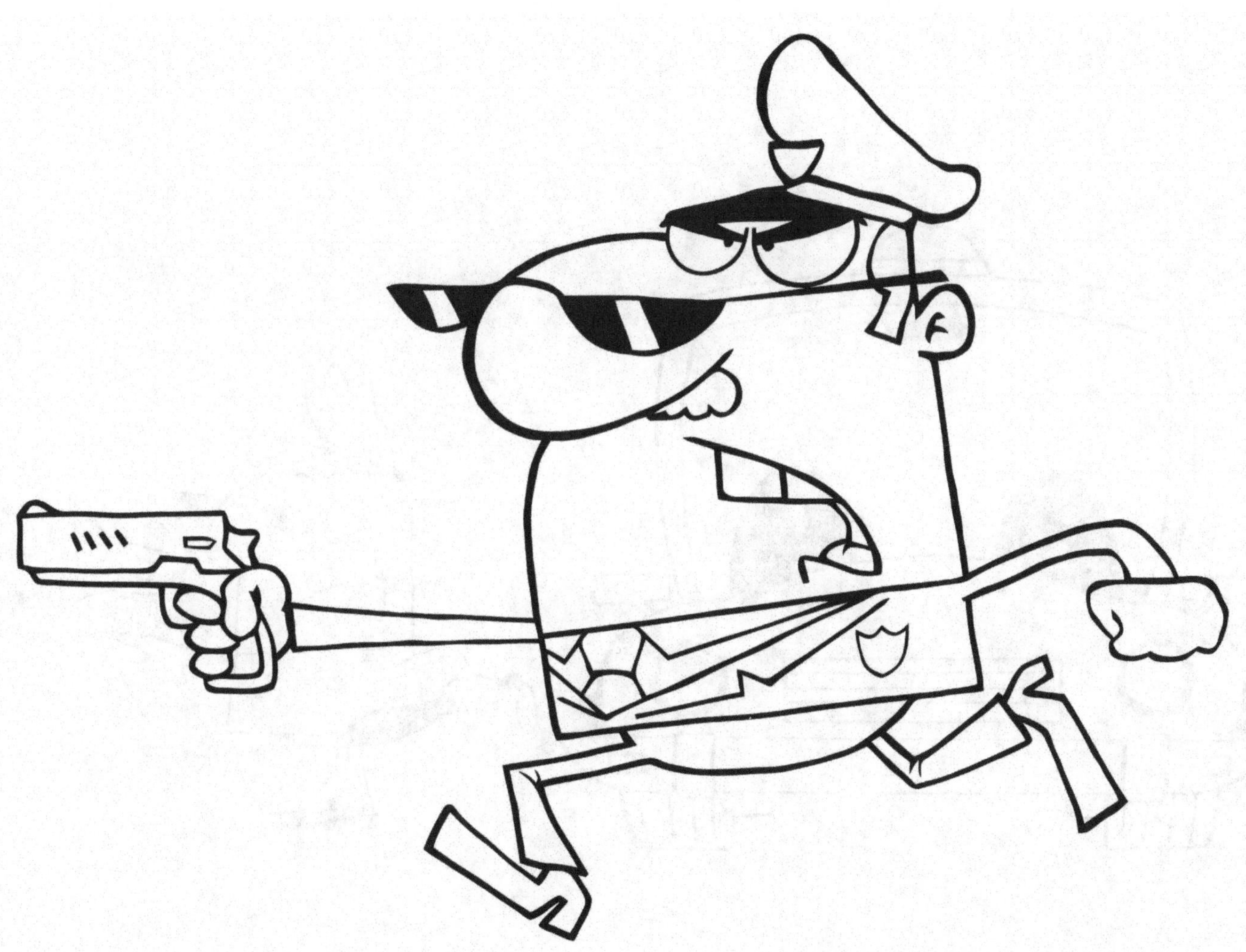

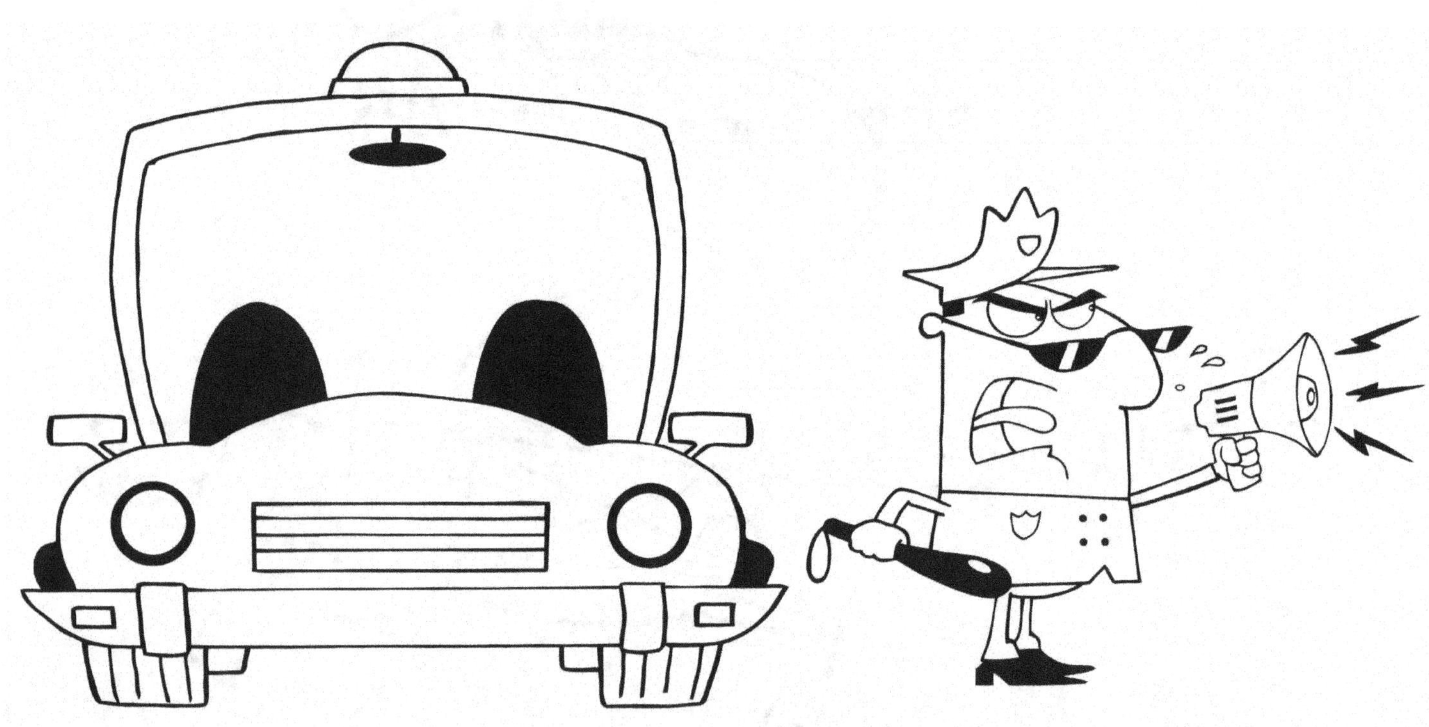

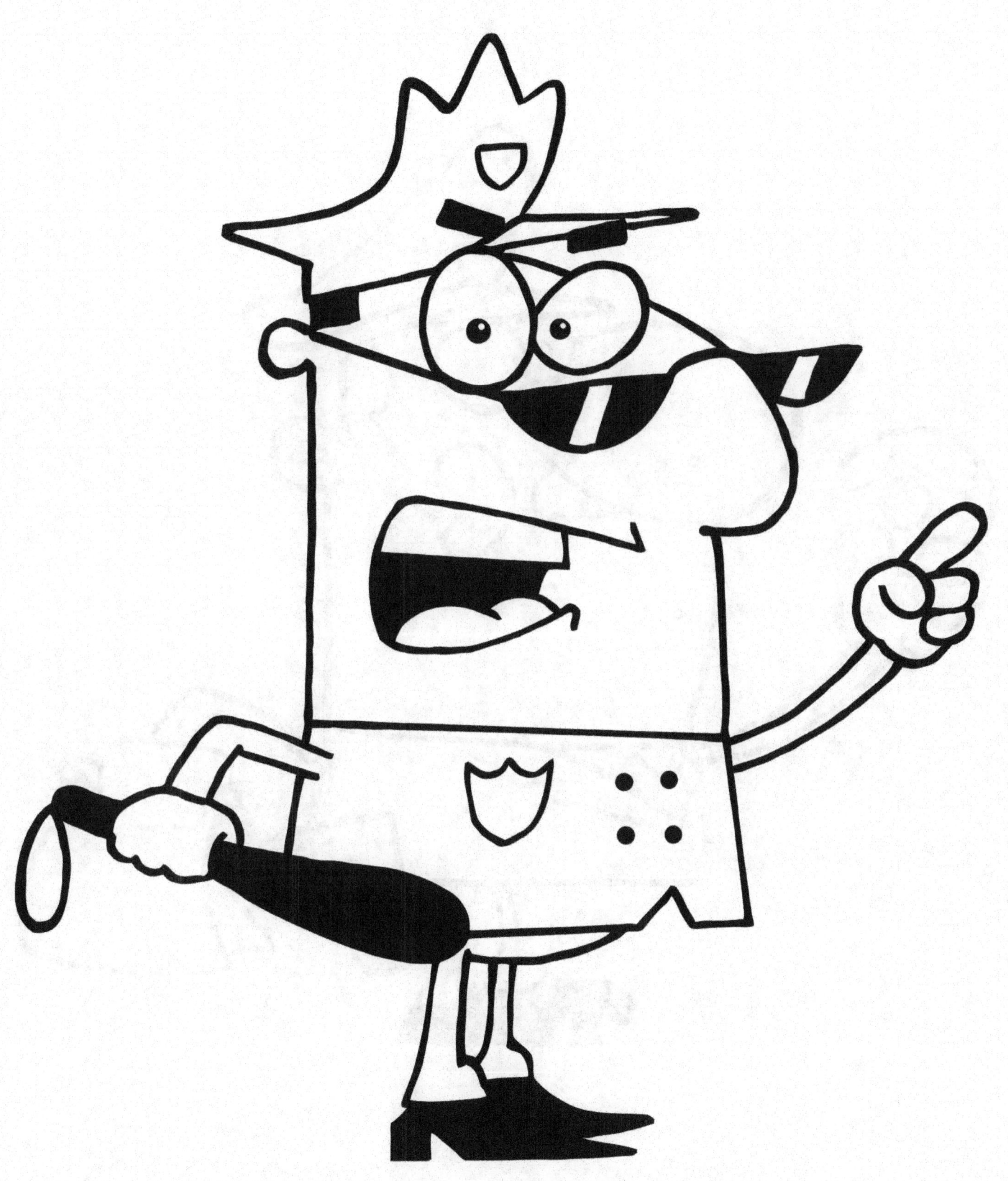

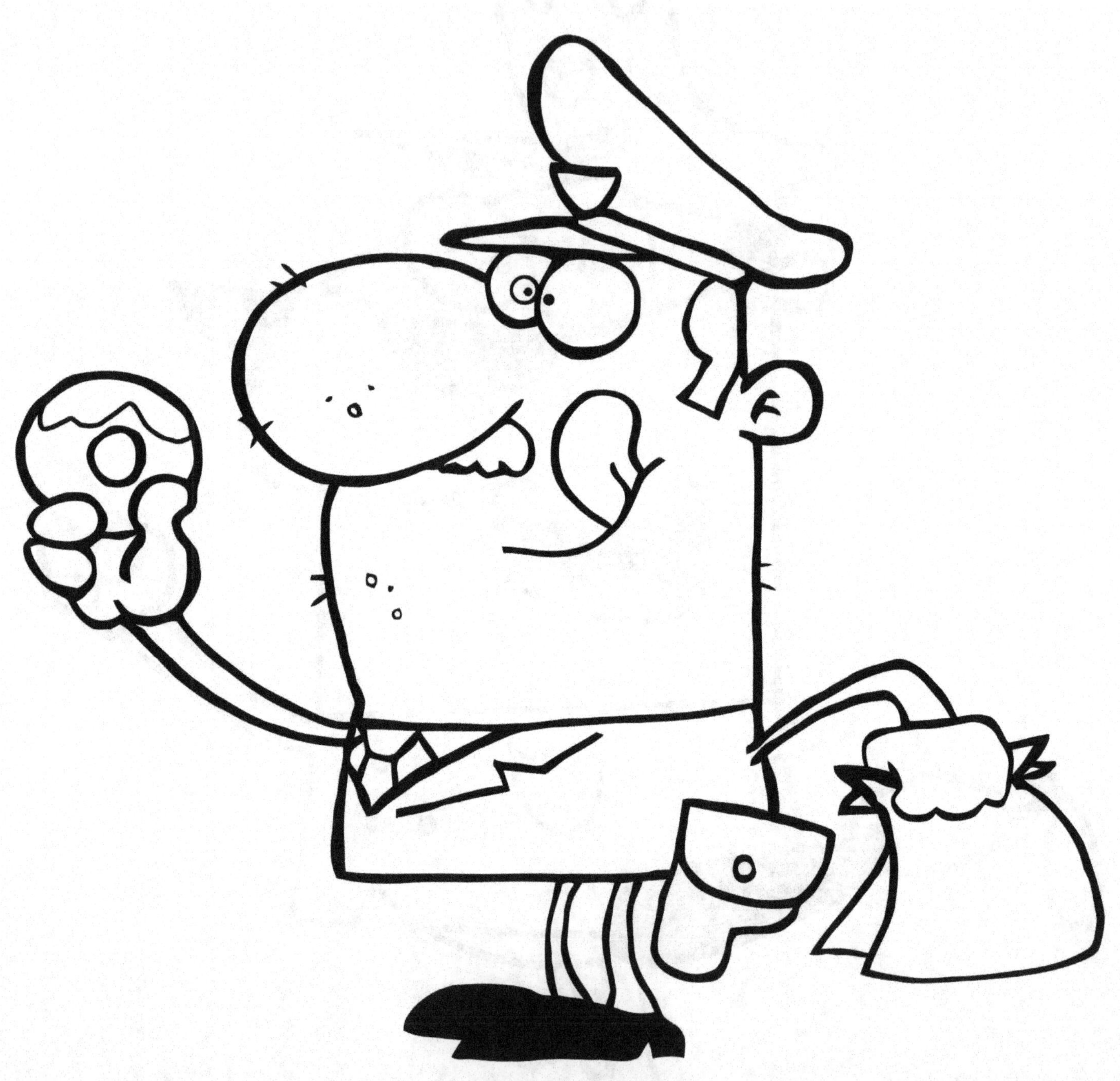

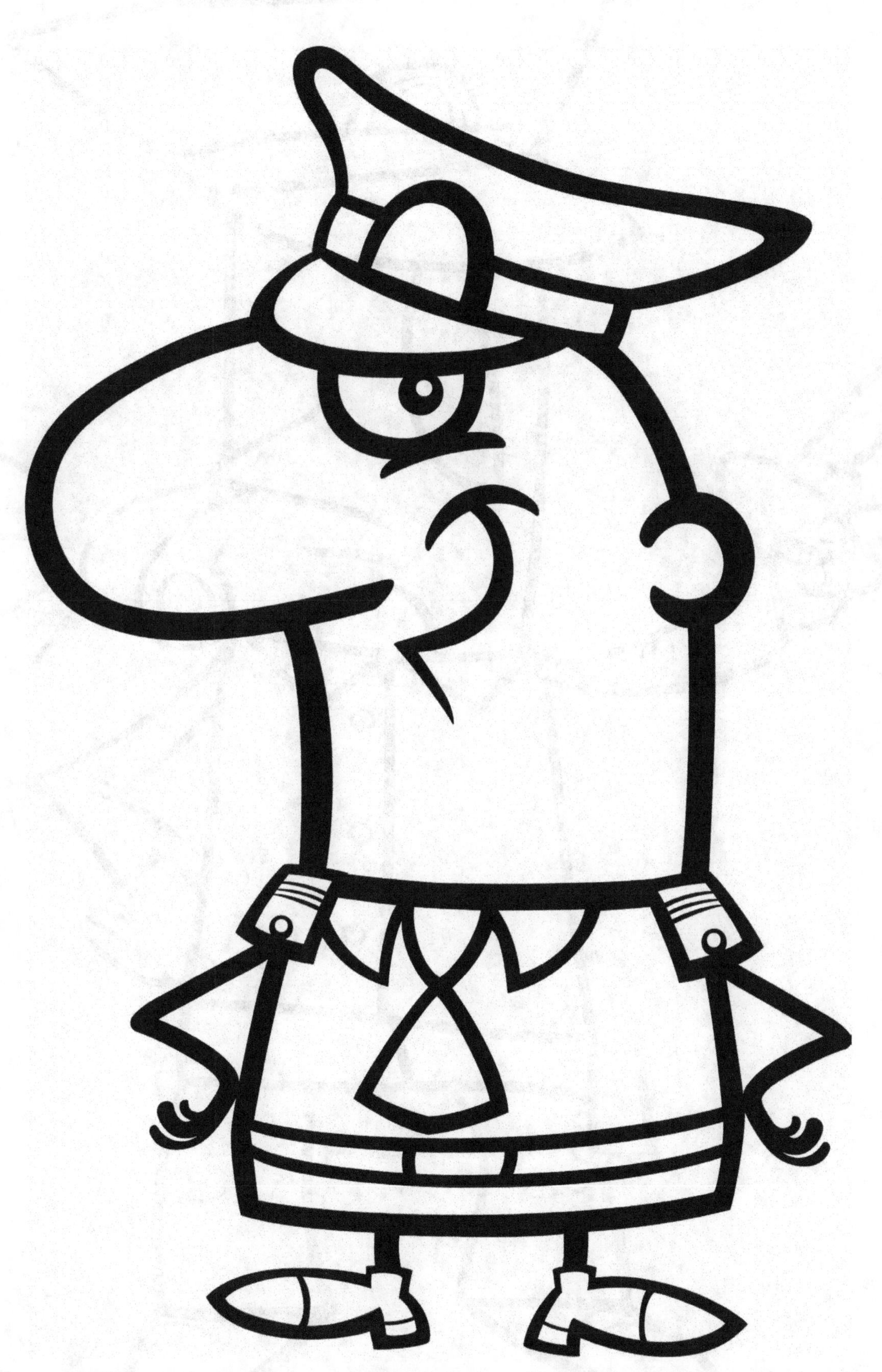

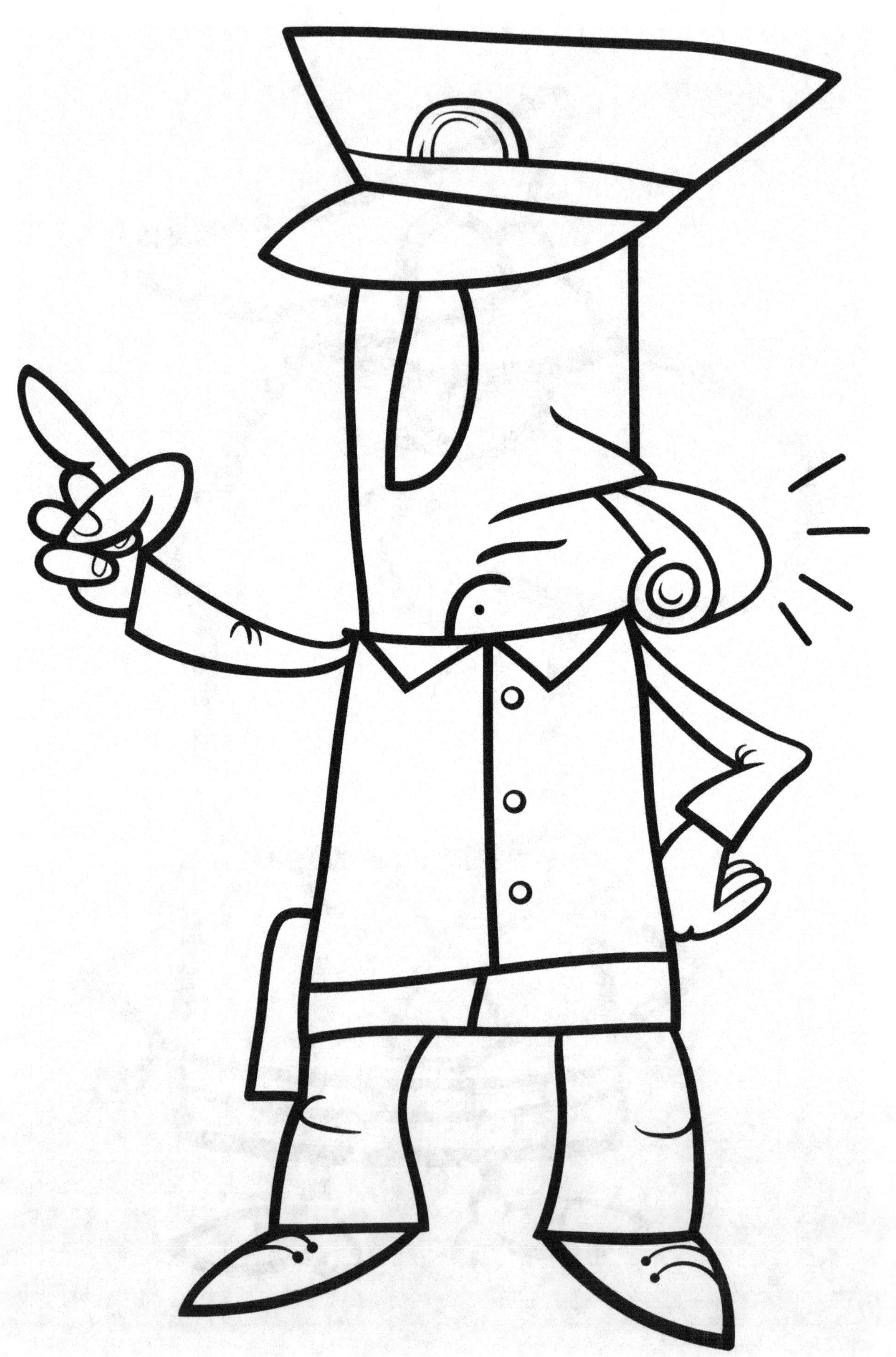

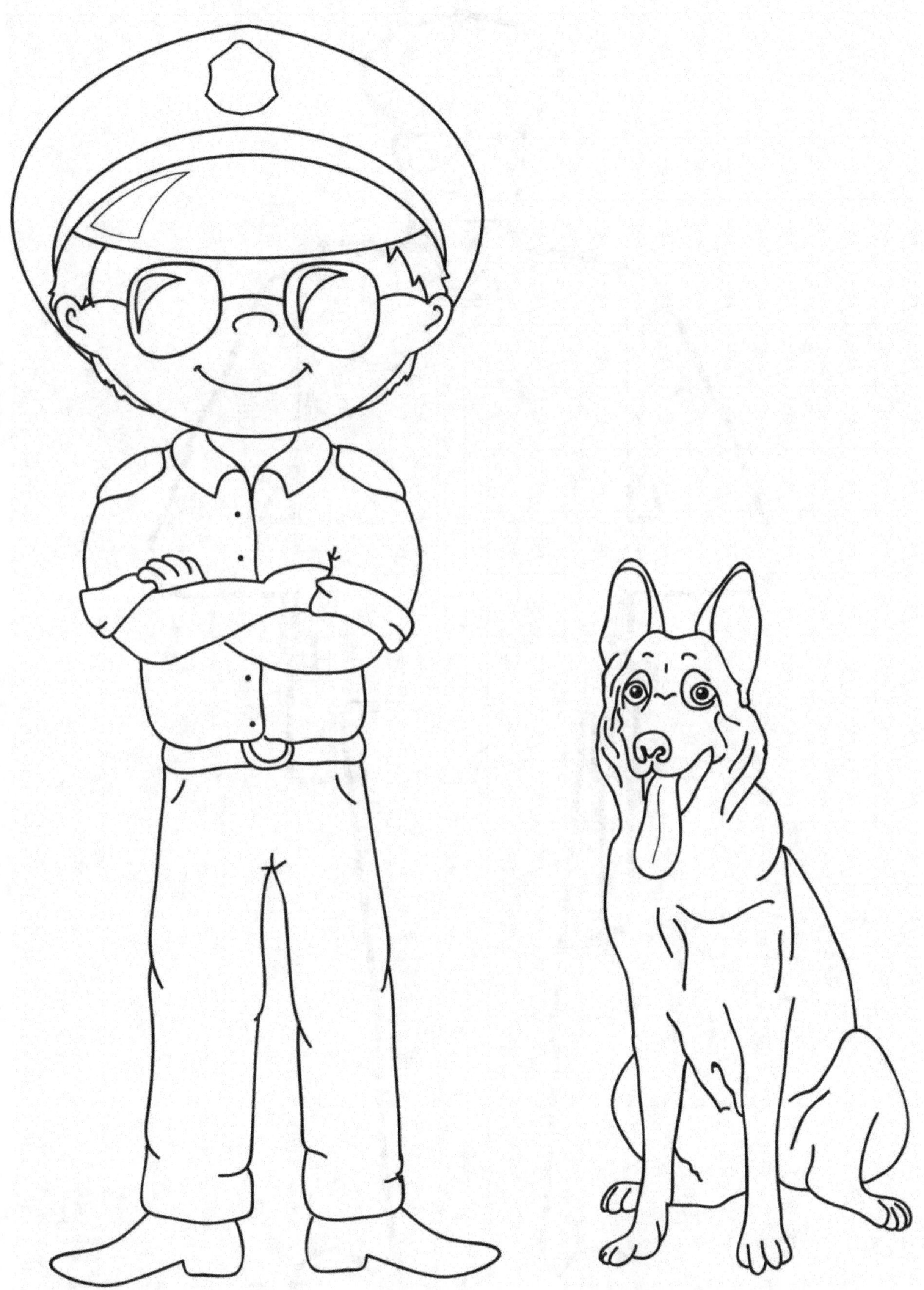

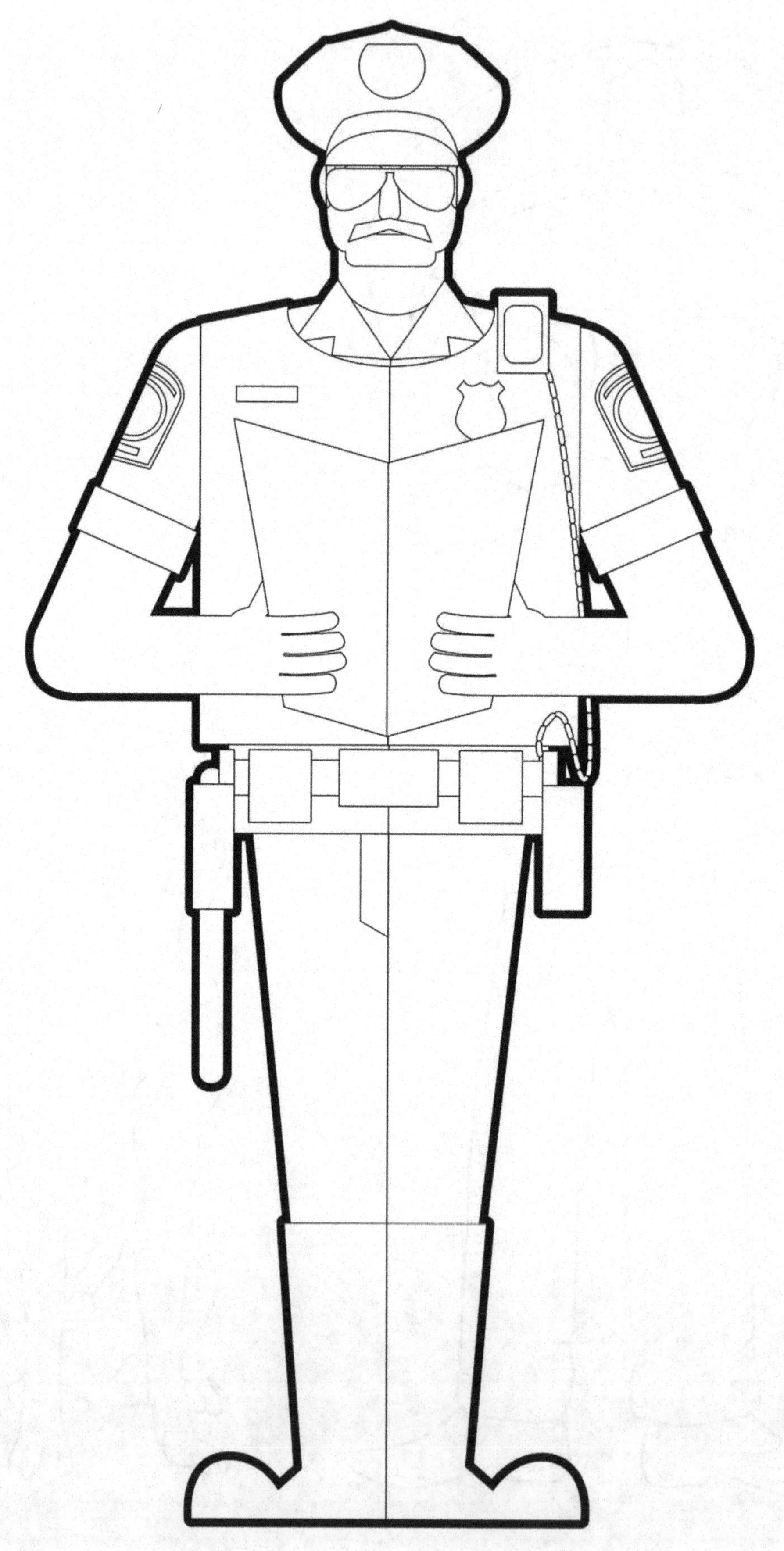

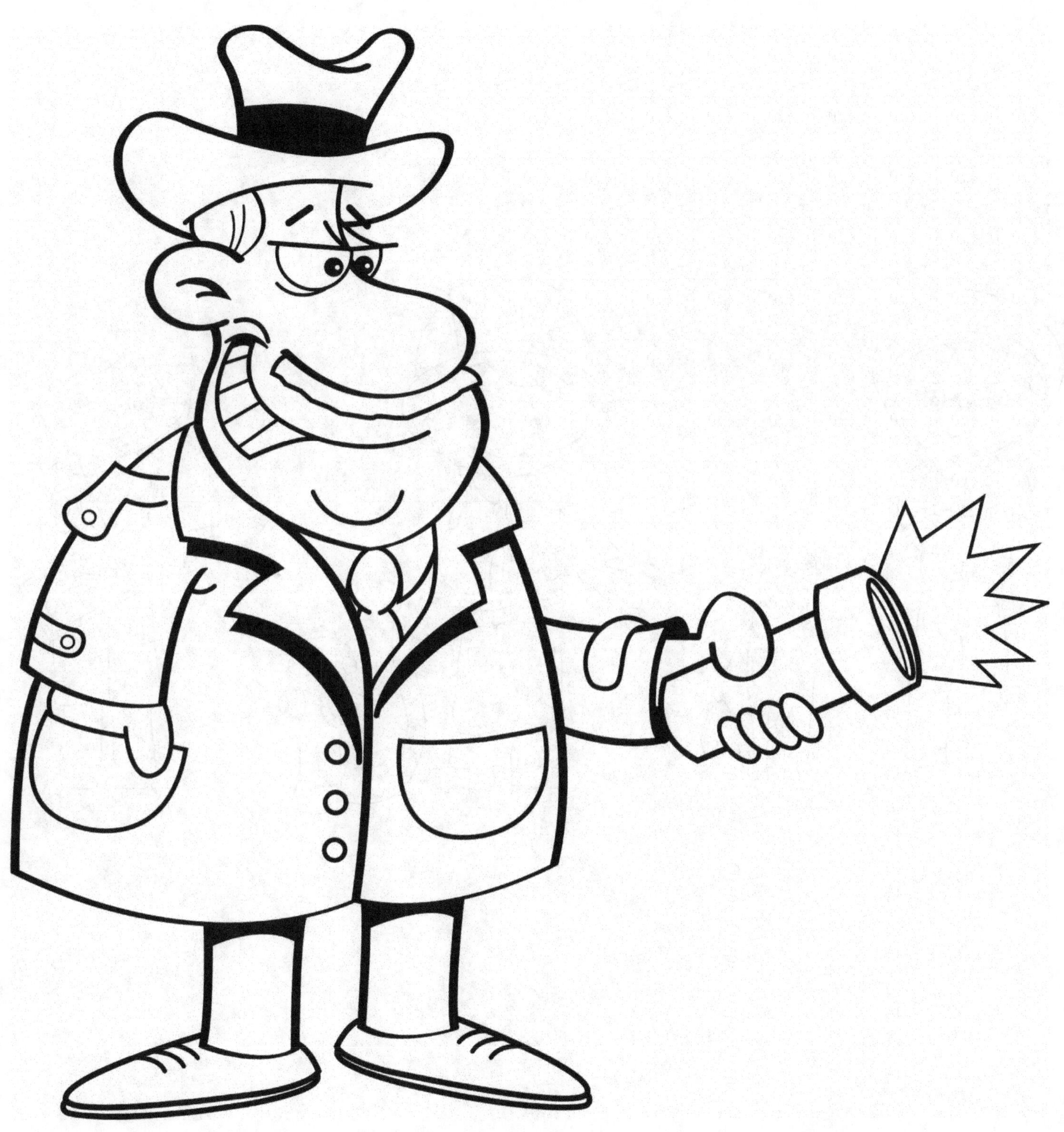

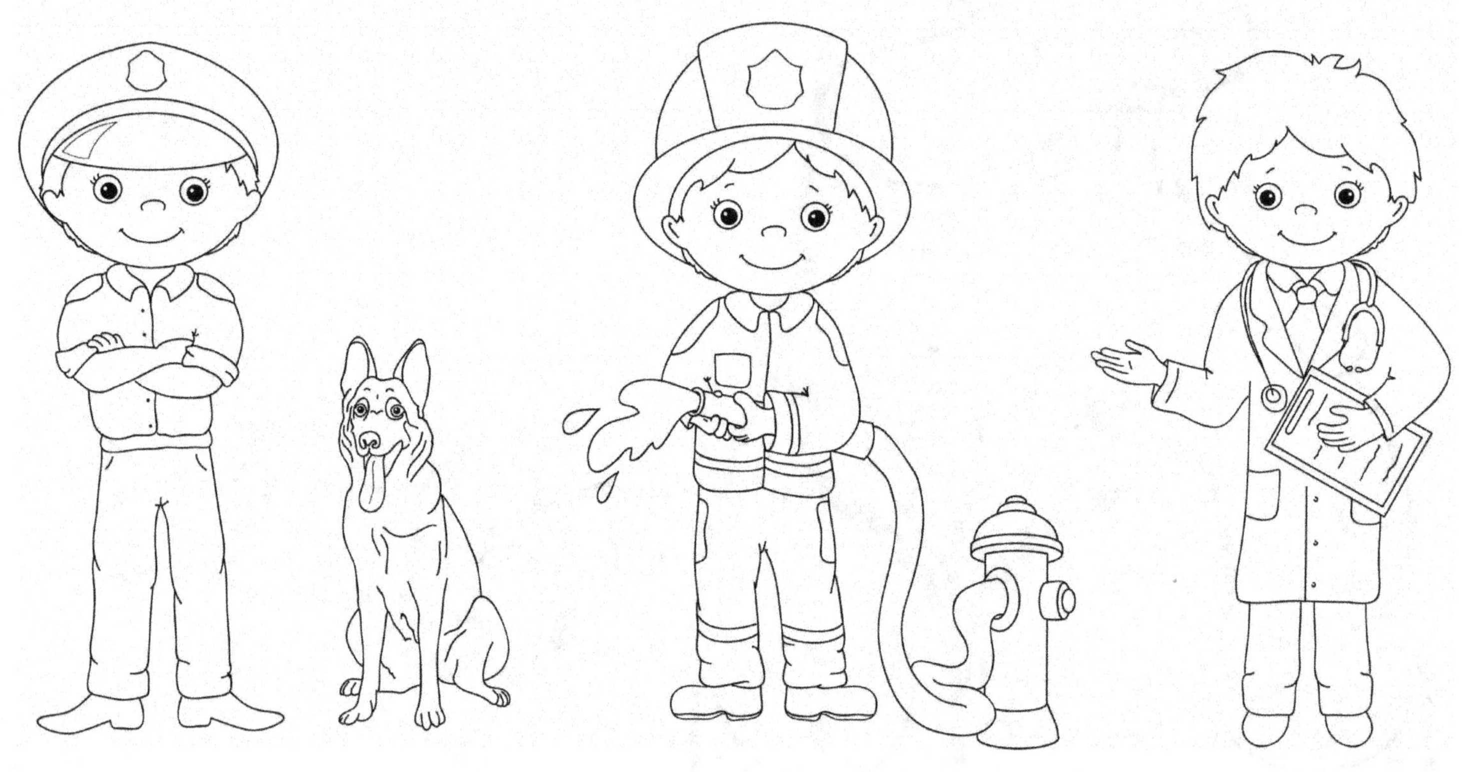

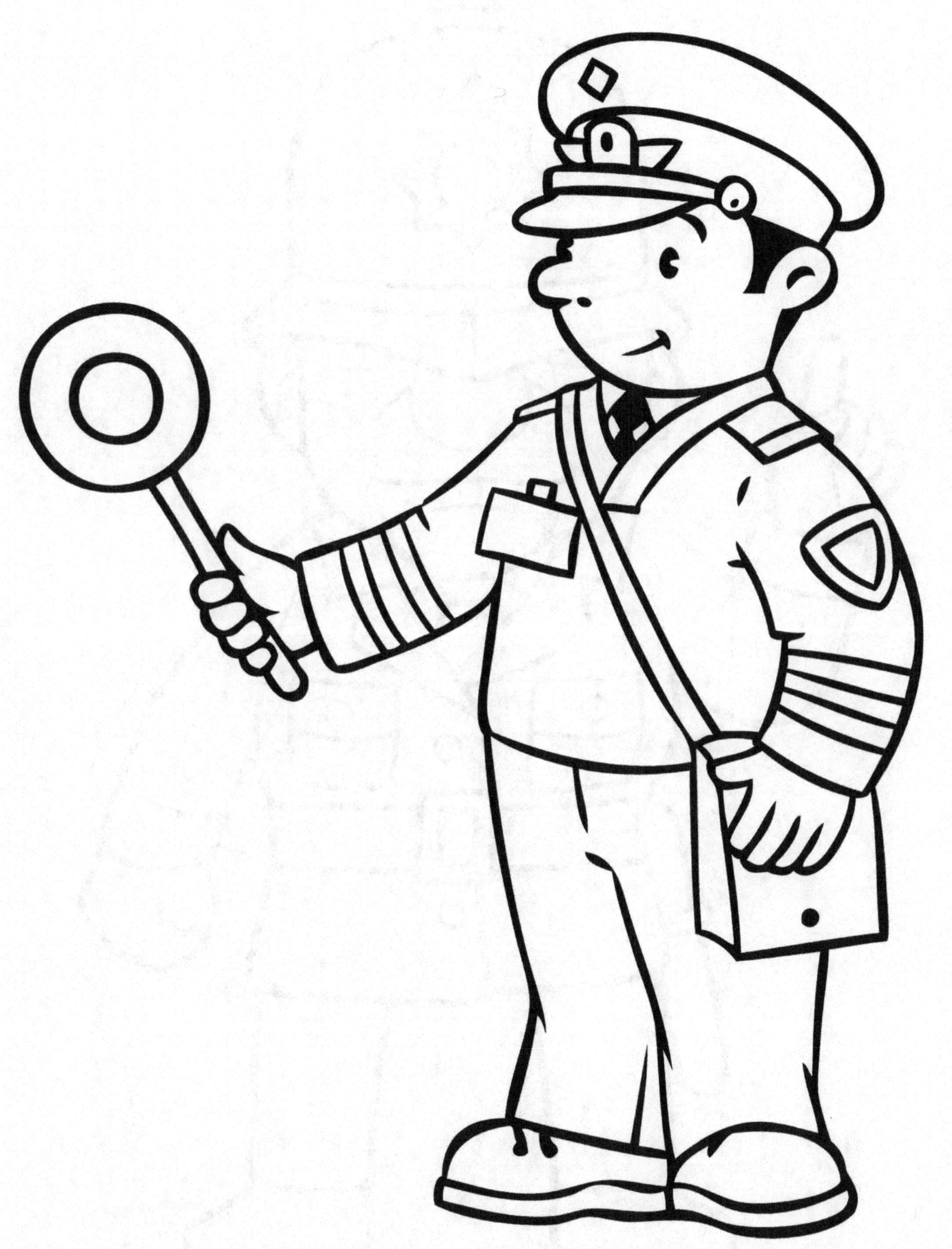

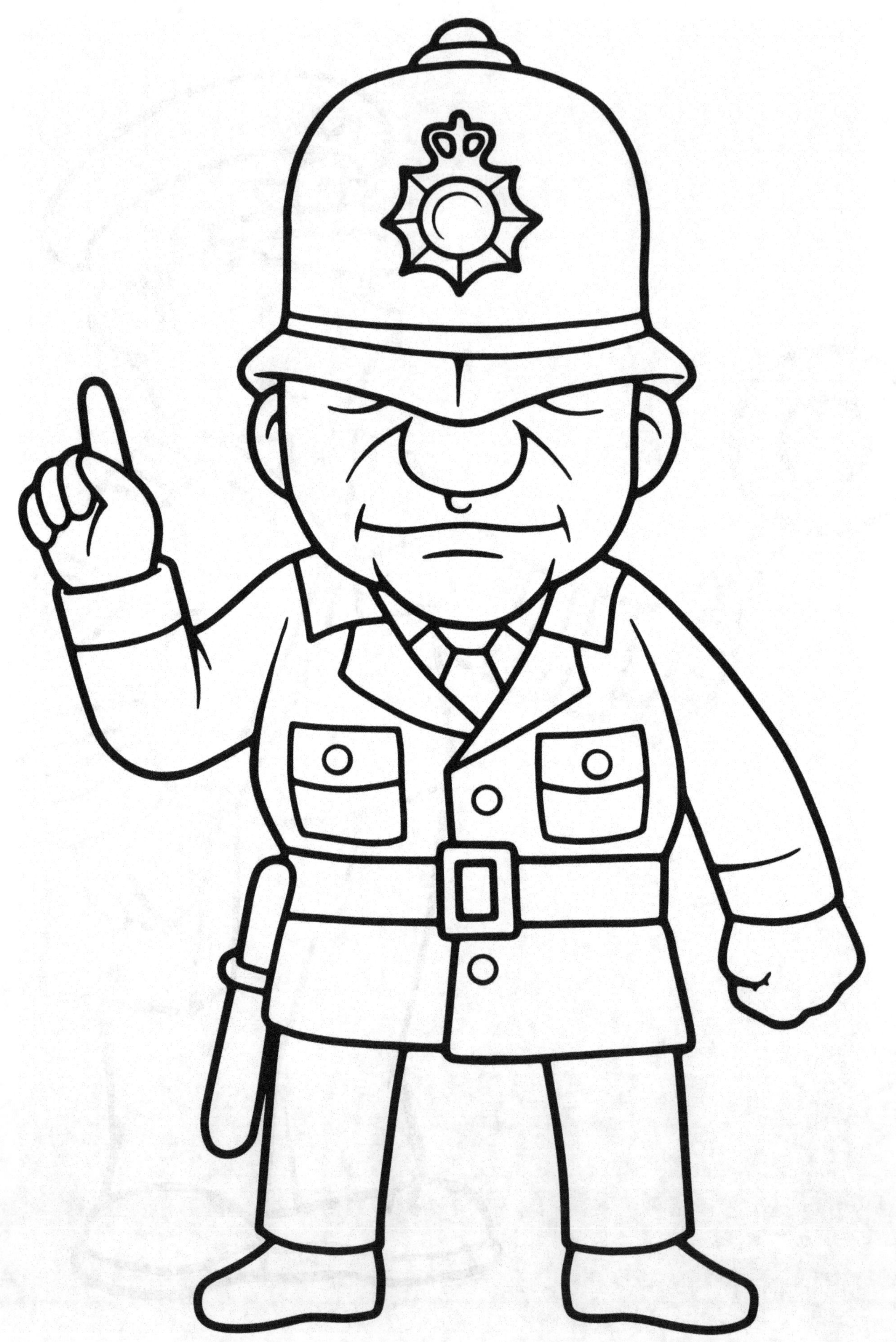

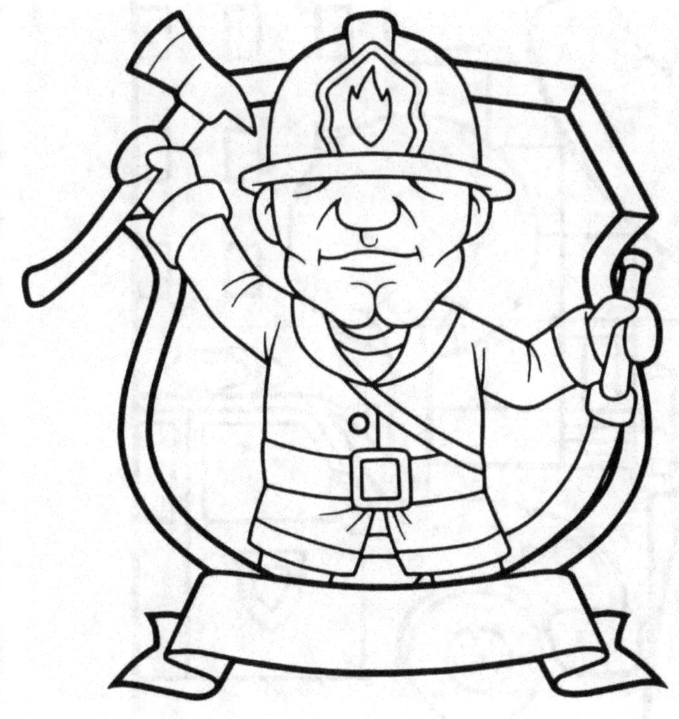

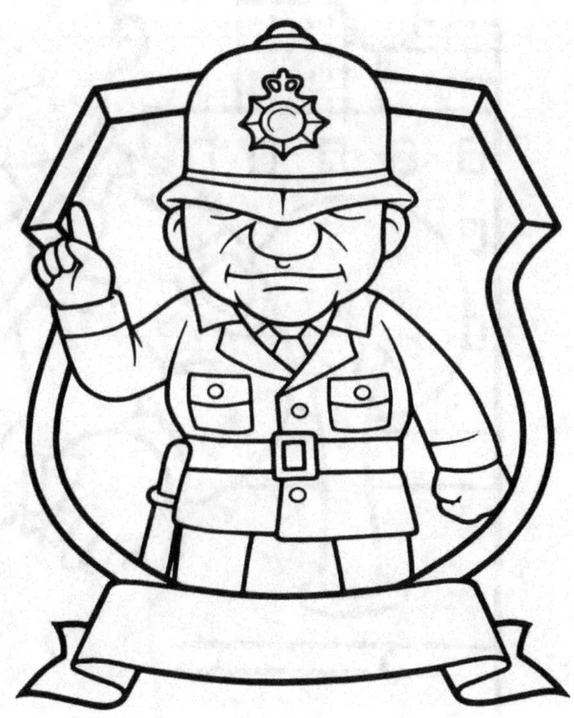

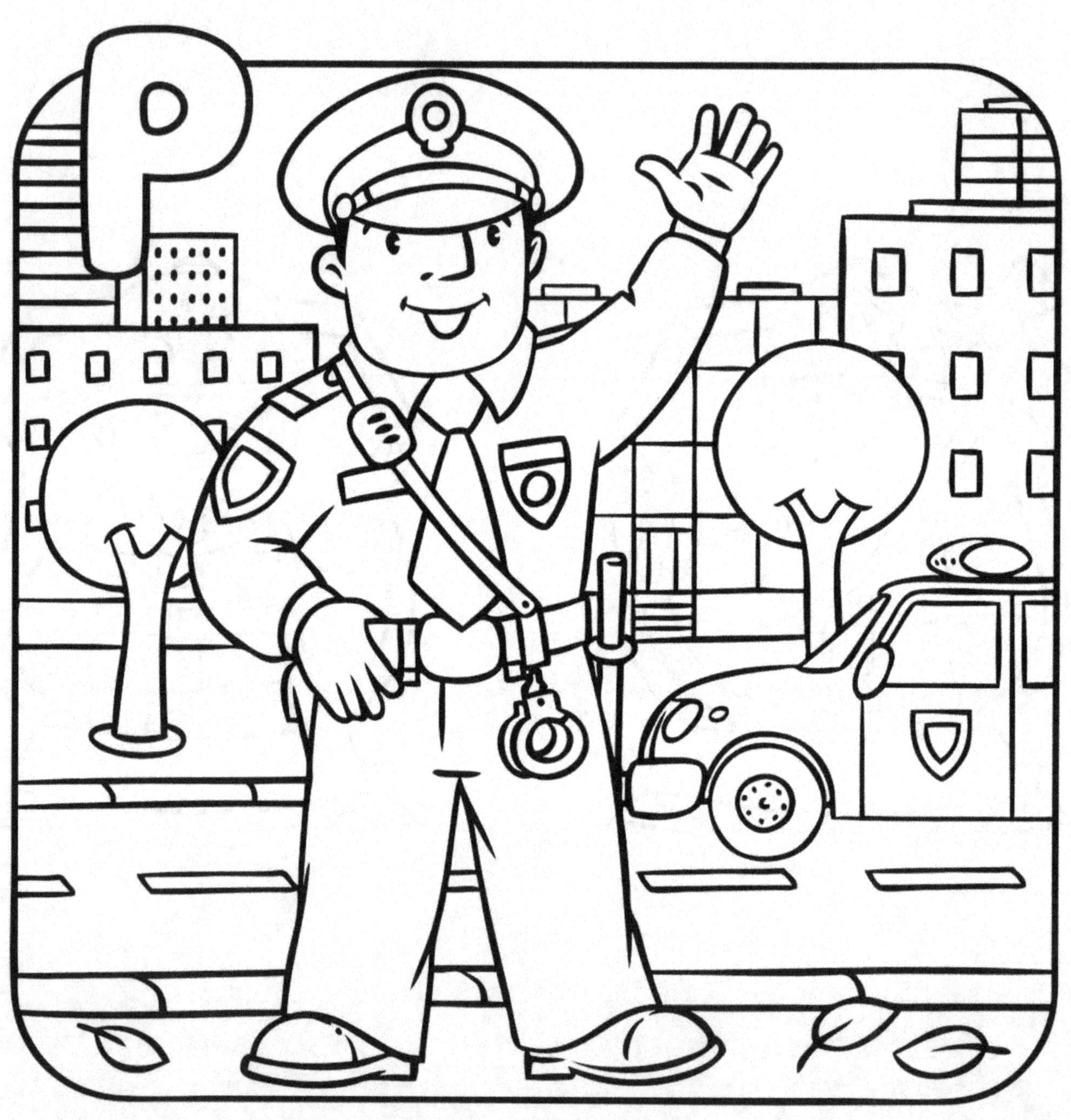

P

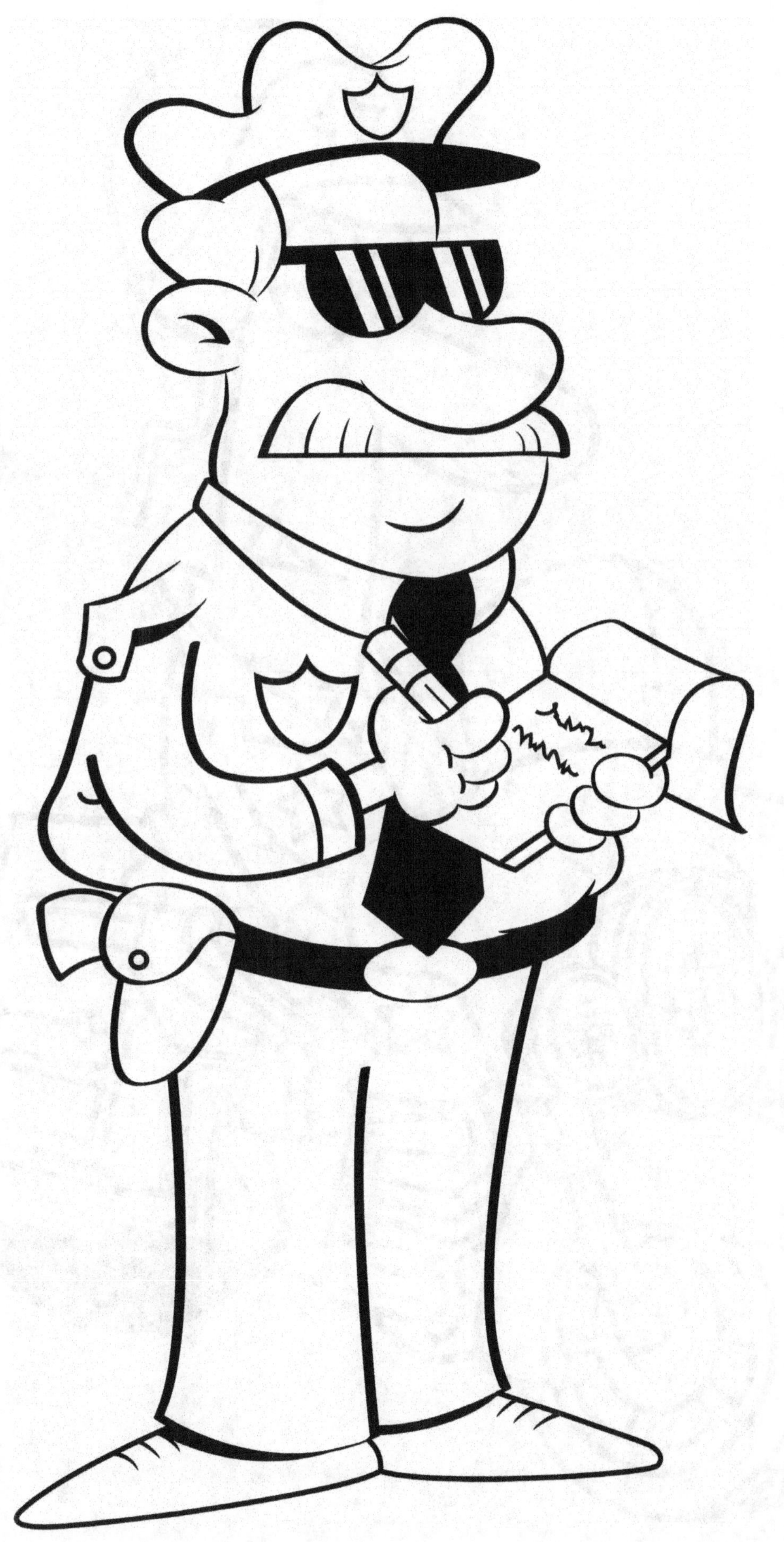

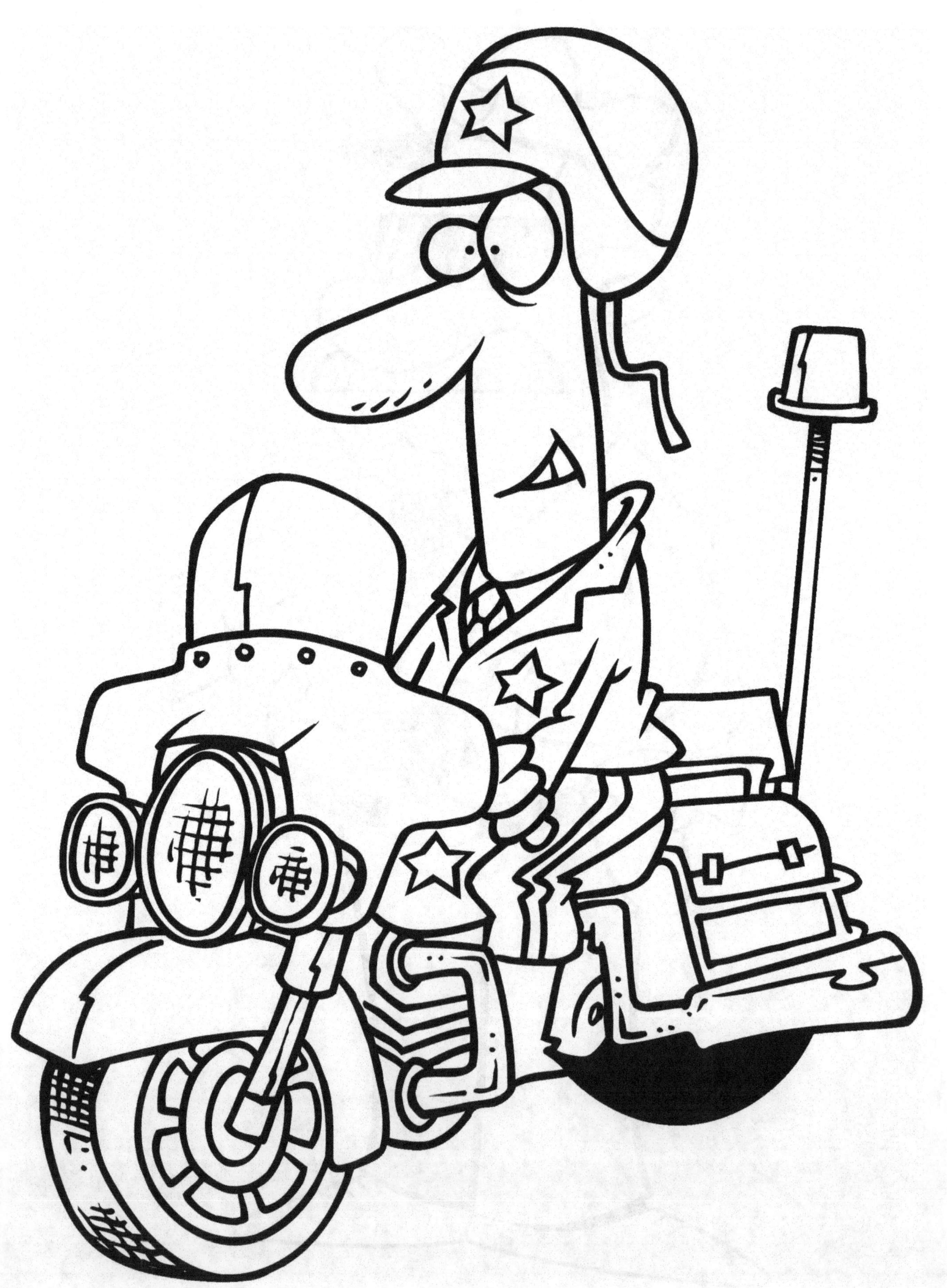

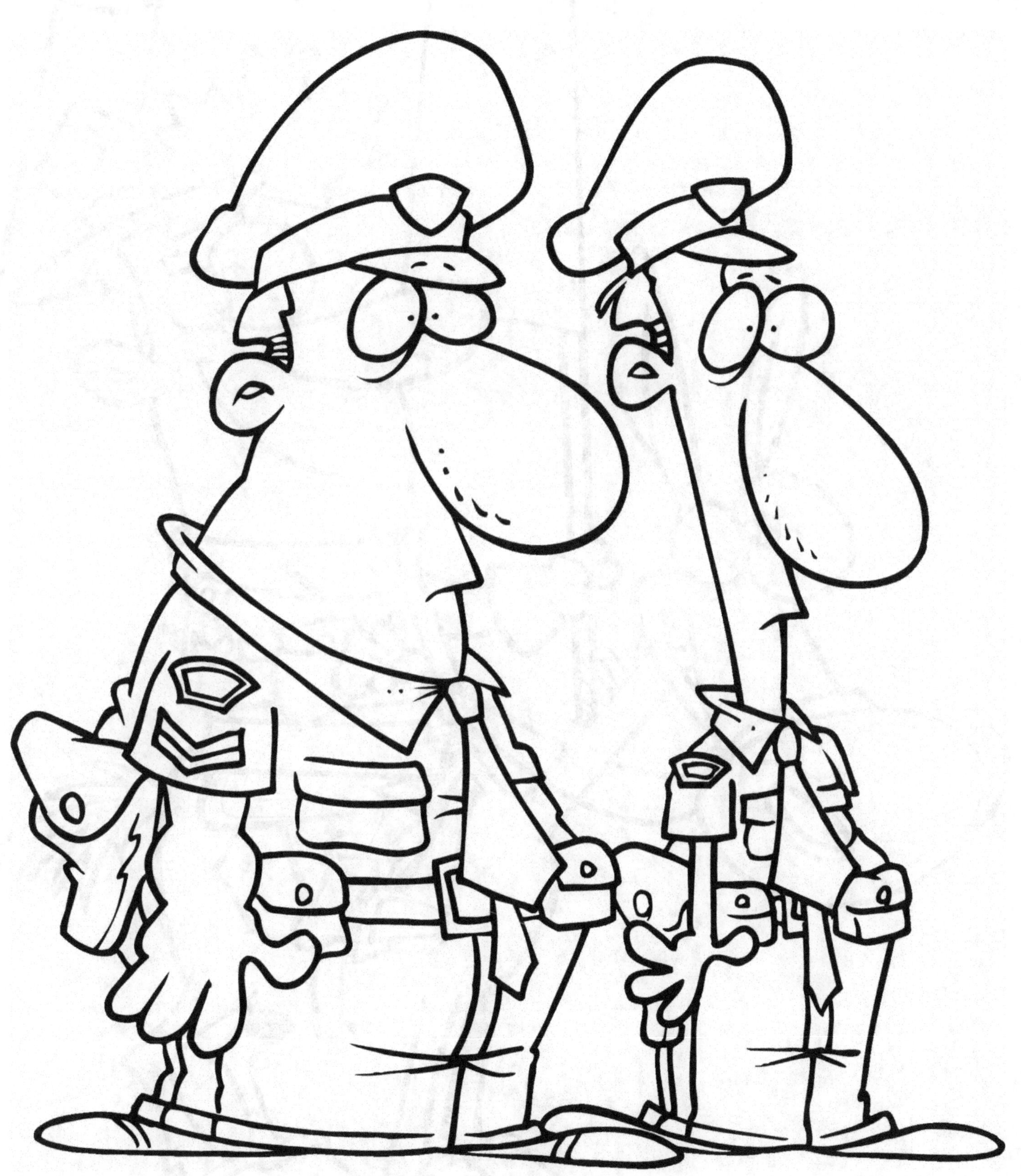

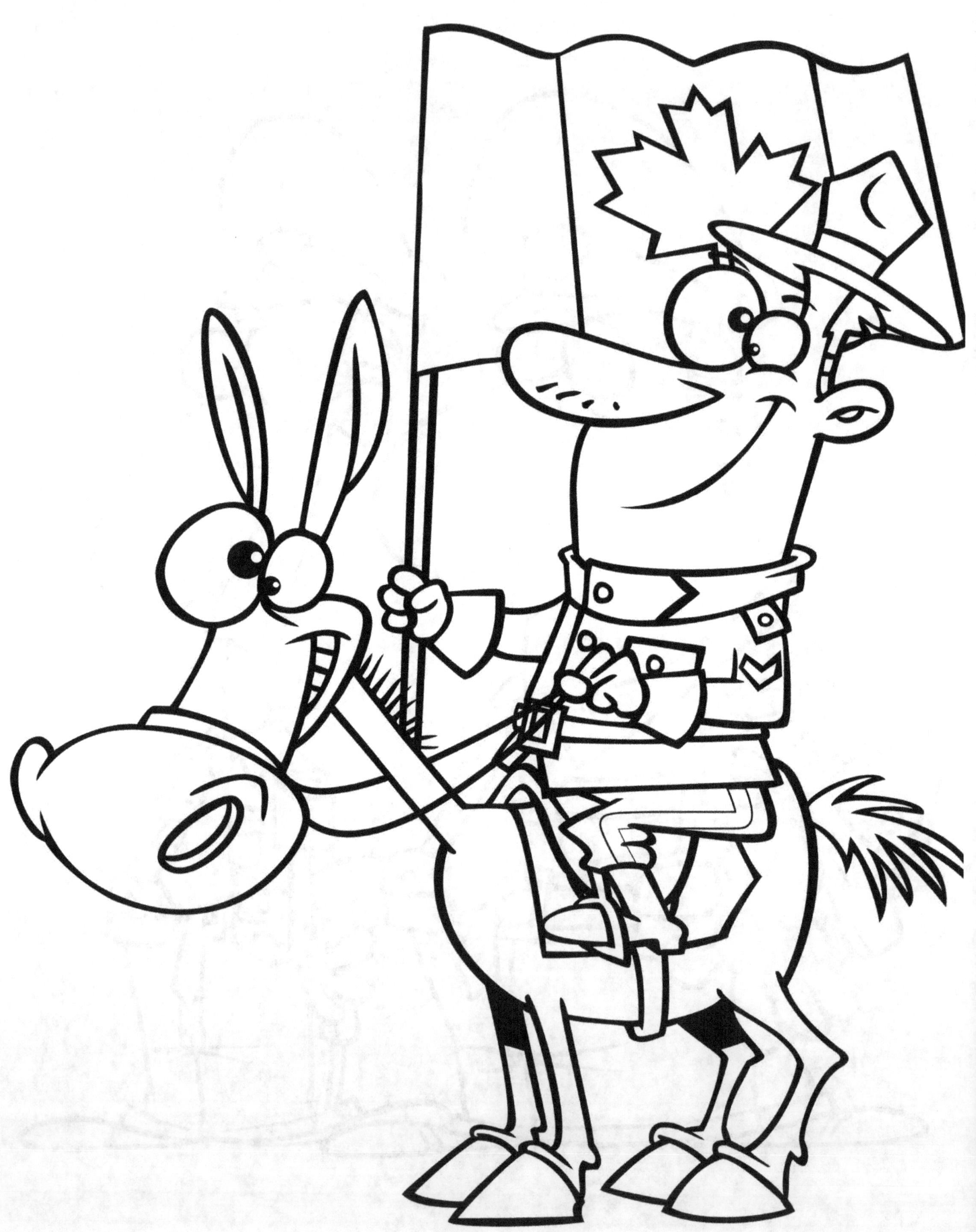

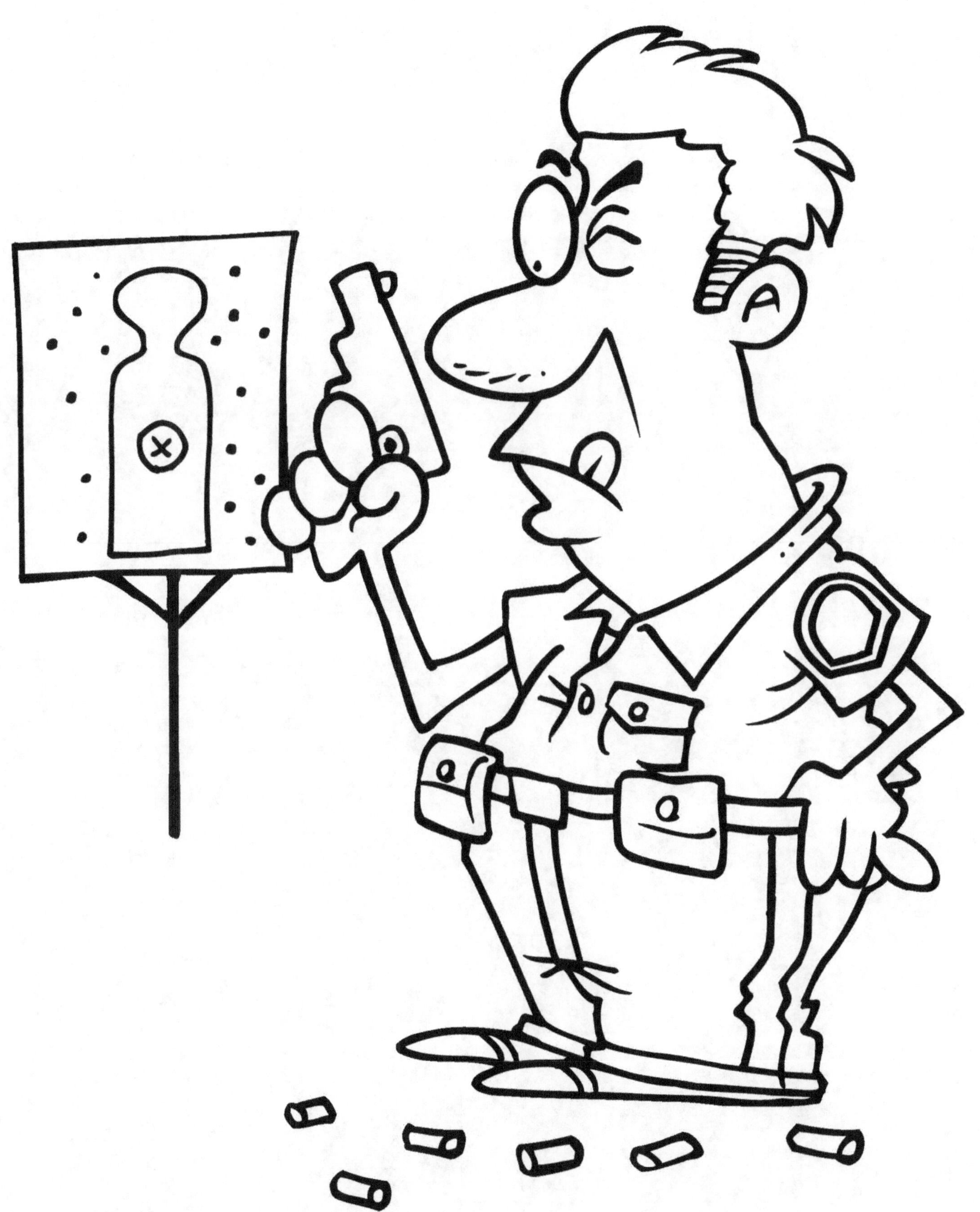